THAT'S THE KINGDOM OF GOD

A FRESH LOOK AT THE KINGDOM
AND OUR PLACE IN IT

BY
STAN E. DEKOVEN, PH.D.

For information on reordering, or to obtain
a catalog of other books by Dr. DeKoven
and other related resources, please contact:

Vision Publishing
1520 Main Street, Suite C
Ramona, CA 92065
(760) 789-4700
www.vision.edu

Table of Contents

For years we (pastors) have focused our attention on building the church increasing our members, having the best worship. However, the focus of Jesus' ministry and the apostles was not on the church, but the Kingdom of God. Perhaps we need to rethink our purpose and practice.

Forward

In a recent exhortation spoken at our church's annual conference, I shared briefly on my perspective on the Kingdom of God and it's presence as far as our life message and ministry focus.

I was reminded as I read Luke 10:1-9 (the sending of the 70) that there were these specific aspects to their responsibility as ministers. First, they were to proclaim peace, second, they were to heal the sick and third, they were to proclaim the Kingdom. The fact is, God's intention is to see the Kingdom rule everywhere. What man lost in the Garden through sin, the loss of dominion; (Adam was driven from God's Kingdom, the garden), God has restored (or at least is restoring) through Christ's death and resurrection. Essentially, God is in the business of the restoration of His Kingdom, having given dominion to His church.

Thus, our lives, our churches, our ministries are not about the church, but about the Kingdom of God, not about our destination (heaven, big church, whatever) but about the journey, in the Kingdom, the King. For He shall reign forever and ever and His reign began on the Day of Pentecost and will continue and expand until the gospel has been preached to all nations then the end shall come.

So much could be said about Christ and His Kingdom. In this book, Dr. DeKoven presents with clarity and conviction the certainty of the Kingdom for all time. It will whet your appetite and expand your thoughts beyond the church to God's rule everywhere.

Dr. Joseph Thornton
Liberty Church Fellowship

Author's Foreword

It wasn't until a conversation after a pastor's prayer meeting that I gave serious thought to the importance of the Kingdom of God. The leader of the prayer gathering and I began a long and profitable discussion, which has lead to a passionate pursuit of all things Kingdom.

As a young man, my focus of Christian life vacillated between a desire to win souls individually, with the Four Spiritual Laws booklet, and holding on to escape the tribulation (the Rapture). My belief at the time, immature as it was, was that the Kingdom of God was delayed, that it was for the future millennial reign of a 1000 years. Like many, I was taught and firmly believed that the Jewish believers without the presence of the Holy Spirit (who would leave with the church 7 years earlier) would somehow establish the Kingdom of our Lord and of His Christ to reign forever.

It took several years of research into scripture to convince me that my earlier, most sincere but incomplete teaching on the kingdom was more than misinformation. The former teaching actually took from me a clear understanding of God's ultimate purpose in the earth. The Kingdom of God is not future but was inaugurated by Christ, is administered on the earth by the Holy Spirit, and will ultimately be consummated when Christ returns at the end of the age.

My purpose for writing this book is to present some of the key elements of the Kingdom of God for practical daily usage. The Kingdom of God, though vital in our understanding is not a monolithically difficult construct to grasp.

All believers have been born again in order to enter the Kingdom of God, understand its principles, and function as full-fledged members of His awesome, dynamic and conquering Kingdom. Understanding our place and function in God's wonderful Kingdom is a key to fulfilling our purposes for Christ in the earth.

Acknowledgements

The desire to write on this important subject has been with me for some time. There have been many influences of a most positive nature who have with their life and unique perspective on Christendom contributed to my thinking and keen interest. These include Dr. Joseph Thornton and Dr. Kathryn Thornton, Pastors of Liberty Christian Fellowship in Fresno California, who so freely shared their loving friendship and unique perspective until the light went on for me. Further, I am most grateful to Rev. George Runyan of San Diego City Church Ministries, a church planting apostle and pastor who through weekly dialog has helped me clarify my thinking, and whose friendship is most liberating. He and the rest of our Thursday morning prayer group have expanded my vision for the church in the city.

Of course, I have been so very blessed with a loving and supportive family, including my first wife Karen (who passed away in 2000), and my beautiful wife Noreen, a gift from God. I also thank my equally beautiful daughters Rebecca and Rachel, and my parents Ron and Louise DeKoven (deceased 2002). They have graciously tolerated my at times over zealousness to see the Kingdom expanded in less than supernatural fashion. Thank you all for your patience.

Finally, this book is dedicated to the Lord Jesus and His church, the agent, by the power of the Holy Spirit on earth for the expansion and management of His Kingdom. It is my hope that this volume will inspire, encourage and expand Kingdom awareness as we all prepare the Bride for the final return of the King for His Bride.

"The Kingdom of God is not realm but reign;
not domain but dominion."

- William Newton Clarke

That's The Kingdom of God
Introduction

God is doing wonderful things around the world! He is renewing and refreshing worldwide, repairing, restoring, and equipping people to do greater things for God than ever before.

His church has been sour for a long time, filled with people carrying heavy weights and unnecessary grief. Yet they haven't known how to lay these burdens down. The renewal that God has brought has been experienced by many as rivers of God beginning to flow. The rivers are chipping away at the debris that has settled in the streams of our hearts. People have not necessarily fasted, prayed, or cried out to God for renewal; our God has acted sovereignly. God has chosen to begin His renewal, because of His love for His people.

God is cleaning and preparing His Bride for a specific purpose in these last days. Of course, no one knows how long those last days will last. We do know that the Kingdom of God will continuously expand and grow. People around the world are being saved, healed, and delivered. God is doing it sovereignty, wonderfully, out of His grace and mercy. One manifestation of His expanding Kingdom has been described as holy laughter. Whether holy or not could be debated. There is nothing new under the sun. I experienced abundant joy 25 years ago. Prior to that, people who were part of the Latter Rain movement experienced similar phenomena, including shaking and quaking. Whether this latest refreshing is a true revival or not, only time will determine. I am certain that lives are changing, God is moving, and the Kingdom of God will continue to expand as we activate our renewed lives into evangelistic fervor.

God is preparing His Bride for a specific purpose.

This book contains a series of teachings on the Kingdom of God. It will focus on Romans 14:13-19, the Apostle Paul's perception or perspective on that which was important regarding God's Kingdom. We will look at the Kingdom, and more specifically the three components that Paul talks about in Romans 14:17 "*...for the kingdom of God is not eating and drinking, but righteousness and peace and joy in the Holy Spirit.*" It is my prayer that the body of Christ, and the reader in particular, would experience God's righteousness, peace and joy, that the Lord Jesus would be Lord of the church, and that God's Kingdom would be established amongst us here and now.

"Whenever God rules over the human heart as King, there is the kingdom of God established."

- Paul W. Harrison

Chapter I
Defining the Kingdom
A Starting Place

Many writers have attempted to define the Kingdom of God. The simplest definition and perhaps the best is that the Kingdom of God is the extension of the rule of God throughout the universe. Zorn defined the Kingdom of God this way, "In the broadest sense, God's Kingdom refers to the most extended reaches of His sovereignty (PS. 103:10). Most scholars would agree that the Kingdom of God refers to His reign or rule rather than a sphere, place or domain.

The Kingdom of God is not merely eschatological, but also ever present. Some are looking for the Kingdom of God or the Kingdom of Heaven in the sweet bye and bye, whereas my perspective is that the Kingdom of God has been here since the time of John the Baptist, and is ever expanding. The agency for the expansion of the Kingdom of God is the church.

Others have defined the Kingdom as the territory, or area in which a king rules and reigns. It is an area or sphere in which one holds a preeminent position. Jesus' primary domain or the place He exercised His authority was here in His earthly ministry.

Finally, (though this book nor any other will be the final word on the subject) the Kingdom of God can refer to the complete or consummate purpose of God, His desire and pleasure fulfilled from time and eternity.

Regardless the definition, the Kingdom of God and its ultimate expression and fulfillment is the central theme of all scripture. The plan of the Father to sum up all things in Christ, in Heaven and in earth, is an expression of God's intention to fulfill His purpose and establish His Kingdom forever. This would ultimately be accomplished because of the covenant promise of God that all nations would be blessed through Abraham (Gen. 15).

The establishment of the Kingdom can be seen in the commission of the Lord to mankind as found in the Garden story. Through the Image of God manifested, and the Likeness of God expressed, the Dominion of God would be established through the joint ministry of the man and woman. Of course, the ability to properly rule as God would was lost due to the entrance of sin, polluting all that God desired. Yet, His plan for a Kingdom rule by man under His sovereignty was never altered.

**The Kingdom of God is the extension of the rule
of God throughout the universe.**

In the life of Abraham, another picture of the progression toward the kingdom is presented. Galloway and Galloway provide some insight here, and the importance of the ministry of Moses in the development of the Kingdom in the life of the people of God. They state "As Abraham was the beginning and Father figure of our faith, Moses was the link between Abraham and the living faith of Israel as through Moses God chose to inaugurate the Passover, to lead God's people in the Exodus, and to reveal God's divine Law in covenant with the Chosen people. All of this history and tradition was basic to the teaching of Jesus about the Kingdom of God." Further, David established the heart of the Kingdom and the King, as seen in I Chronicles 28 and 29, where he reveals his desire and plan to build a permanent resting place for God in the Temple. The Temple, and the prosperity of Israel under Solomon provide a view of the splendor of the Kingdom in picture, though it is not the ultimate expression.

Finally, it is in the Prophets (Isa. 2:2-3, 9:2-7, 11:1-11, Jer. 31:31-33) that the future physical and spiritual Kingdom is discussed as a Messianic promise to be shared by the covenant people of God. Especially in Isaiah, important pictures of the Kingdom and its future expression are presented. In Isaiah 9: 2-7 it reads;

> *"The people who walk in darkness (the Gentiles, all nations) will see a great light; Those who live in a dark land, The light will shine on them. Thou shalt increase their gladness; They will be glad in Thy presence as with the gladness of harvest, As men rejoice when they divide the spoil. For Thou shalt break the yoke of their burden and the staff on their shoulders, The rod of their oppressor (Satan), as at the battle of Midian. For every boot of the booted warrior in the battle tumult, And cloak rolled in blood, will be for burning, fuel for the fire. For a child will be born to us, a son will be given to us; And the government (authority to rule,*

power) will rest on His shoulders; And His name will be called Wonderful Counselor, Mighty God, Eternal Father, Prince of Peace. There will be no end to the increase of His government or of peace, On the throne of David and over his kingdom, To establish it and to uphold it with justice and righteousness From then on and forevermore. The zeal of the Lord of hosts will accomplish this".

Found amongst many important themes is the purpose for the coming of the Messiah to occupy the throne of David. God's purpose would be the establishment of the government of God on the earth. The authority to accomplish this would be given to Christ, to establish an ultimate rule of justice and righteousness and peace. This would be the very joy of the nations, a theme we will see again in the description of the Apostle Paul to be reviewed in detail later. The Prophet for saw a time when the absolute rule of God would exist, in all its fullness, the beneficiaries of which would be mankind from all nations, a cross-cultural gathering of the haves and the have-nots, the powerful and the weak, the advantaged and disadvantaged, a multi-colored coat of the peoples of the world, occurring through the power of the Holy Spirit (see Isa. 11: 1-10).

From the time of the prophets until the prophet John the Baptist, the expectation of the Kingdom and its manifestation was a Hebrew hope (and for some, remains so). For those who have embraced the message of the Kingdom as preached by the Baptist, established by Jesus, and proclaimed throughout the ages, the Kingdom is an ever present reality, a future hope, an expanding light to the world.

"The kingdom of God does not exist because of your effort or mine. It exists because God reigns. Our part is to enter this kingdom and bring our life under his sovereign will."

- T.Z. Koo

Chapter II
Paul's Perspective
Thoughts on the Kingdom

The Kingdom of God is a vibrant, living expression of God's purpose in the earth. Believers throughout history have wondered about this Kingdom. Perhaps this is why Paul addresses the issue to the church in Rome. Let's look at his discussion leading up to his definition of this marvelous Kingdom.

> *"Therefore, let us not judge one another anymore. But rather determine this..." (Romans 14:13)*

This phrase, "determine this", and the meaning of the phrase, is unfortunately lacking in the church today. Many a believer has failed to make a simple decision, where common sense or a basic understanding of the Word of God would be sufficient with which to decide. Instead, they wait for God to provide a "revelation" or some supernatural sign before moving ahead. Paul seems to be stating that there is a responsibility on the part of the Christian to make some decisions in regard to one's behavior (in this case, that of judging others) that can determine the path of growth or lack thereof. People are saved by grace, through faith. Yet even in salvation, a decision had to be made. If the believer is Charismatic, somehow the determination to be open to receive the baptism of the Holy Spirit, to allow the seemingly foolish activity of speaking in unknown tongues was made. Each week, one must determine to attend church instead of "partying hearty" somewhere else. Paul says: "I want you to determine or firmly establish in your heart something that is probably more important than anything else in your life."

He continues: "Determine not to put an obstacle or a stumbling block in a brother's way. I know and am convinced in the Lord Jesus that nothing is unclean in itself" (Rom. 14:13). Does that sound like a surprising statement? Nothing is unclean in and of itself. The earth is the Lord's, its fullness, and all that it contains (1 Cor. 10:26). Nothing is really unclean, says the Apostle Paul, because everything belongs to the Lord. He's not talking, of course, about the devil or specific evil. One's actions and basic personality style, in and of themselves, are usually quirks of parenting; the combination of environment and genetics. If these things were that changeable, psychologists and sociologists could probably re-engineer the entire world. Nevertheless, God does want His children to determine, or set a course of action in a godly direction and with a Christ like perception to insure that the course of life will be as required by the Lord.

> *"I know and am convinced in the Lord Jesus that nothing is unclean in itself, but to him that thinks anything to be unclean, to him it is unclean. So as a man thinks in his heart, so is he"* (Rom. 14:14).

At times all of God's people are faced with unpleasantness of speech and view. Many of these things are wrong. However, Paul is not referring to areas of sin, which must be dealt with from a biblical perspective. However, what the Word does not prohibit is generally permitted (though

26

it may not be wise, as will be seen later). Thus, a given activity, food to be consumed, clothing to be worn, must be thought through before being judged and condemned. One's heritage or traditions often determine the things that seem unclean or unwise. Paul, as a leader and writer, is attempting to cut away those attitudes that lead towards strife and division. In the church at Rome, there were many issues of unequal treatment between the rich and the poor. The people, including the Spirit-filled leaders, made judgments based upon who was clean or unclean, who was worthy or unworthy. How many Christians understand the dichotomy, that none is worthy but that all of us are worthy in Christ? None is worthy, in and of himself, but all are worthy in Christ because of the blood of Jesus.

> *"For if because of food your brother is hurt, you are no longer walking according to love. Do not destroy with your food him for whom Christ died* (Rom. 14:15).

In other words, you should be mature enough to recognize that other people may be easily offended by things that you allow, and you should be willing to lay them down, at least in front of the one easily offended. Be willing to love enough to not flaunt a given liberty of life style (again, this does not refer to aberrant life styles, such as open fornication or homosexuality, since these are clearly forbidden and condemned throughout the whole of scripture), and cause needless temptation or derision.

"Therefore do not let what is for you a good thing be spoken of as evil. For the Kingdom of God is not eating and drinking, but righteousness and peace and joy in the Holy Spirit" (Rom. 14:16-17).

Thus, Paul presents a contrast in priorities. From a naturalistic perspective, outward appearances and practices seem important, but generally are secondary to inward character; the later being of primary importance and concern.

The earth is the Lord's, its fullness, and all that it contains.

The focus for this book is this, that the Kingdom of God is characterized by righteousness, peace, and joy. These characteristics are to be a part of every believer's life, and are imparted to us by grace through the work of the Holy Spirit in our individual lives. This will be the meat of this study. But first, further discussion on the Kingdom of God itself is in order.

"Blessed are the poor in spirit, for yours is
the kingdom of God"

- Luke 6:20

Chapter III

The Blessed Kingdom

From the time of John the Baptist the Kingdom of God was preached. Jesus also preached it. The Kingdom was the central message that Jesus proclaimed.

"The Kingdom of God is here!" (Luke 17:21)

What did Christ mean by this proclamation? Many people have tried to define this statement; it's really relatively simple. Jesus was saying, *"I'm here; and I am King. Wherever I am, there is My kingdom. And My kingdom is within you, or near to you if you have not yet received Me as your Savior and Lord. I am the King of the Kingdom."* The kingdom of God was near those to whom Jesus and John preached because they had a sense of God's covenant, they understood God's laws and tried to live right. However, behaving properly is not how one enters the Kingdom. Jesus provided the way to enter His kingdom, where He could be the King of ones life, community, and family. It is entered through a decision to receive Christ as savior and Lord, which is also a road of suffering, as spoken of in Acts 14:22.

"Encouraging them to continue in the faith, and saying, 'Through many tribulations we must enter the kingdom of God'" (Acts 14:22).

A true conversion from another religion or none to Christianity sets in motion waves of opposition and problems for the vast majority of believers around the world. The picture often painted in Christian media and even touted from the pulpits of the uninformed is that salvation is a bed of roses with nary a thorn. What rubbish! The call of God to His Kingdom is joyous, provides for peace, and is destined for challenges due to the struggle of sin versus God's word and Satan versus obedience. Though the troubles come, the Lord of the Kingdom provides all that is needed to triumph in spite of the circumstances encountered.

The kingdom is always advancing, even if by force.

> *"From the days of John the Baptist until now the kingdom of heaven suffers violence, and violent men take it by force"* (Mat. 11:12).

Everywhere around the world, people are constantly desiring to press into the kingdom of God, to have and experience what all Christians throughout the ages have had the privilege of experiencing. Sadly, many believers today take for granted the great salvation that is enjoyed so freely. The martyrs of the past and present have given the supreme sacrifice for this freedom so rich. It does God no favor to save mankind from the pit of despair and lift him to the pinnacles of heaven. He did us a grand and glorious favor, based upon His incredible and unfathomable love. He saw the miserable and hopeless waste-of-human-flesh state of man, swooped down, and provided to all the grace and mercy of a perfect provision. All who know the Lord Jesus Christ as Savior have been marvelously chosen by God for His own purpose. Therefore, all allegiance and honor and glory belong to the Lord. Oh, what an awesome God we serve!

Continued Growth

The Kingdom of God continues to grow. For the last ten years, the rate of those being saved around the world is far exceeding the death rate. God is endeavoring to use all of His children in that process. People are being swept into the Kingdom of God now, like never before. Two thirds of the world live in Asian nations. They are desperate to receive the Gospel, and are pressing in. They have tried Communism, Shintoism, Buddhism, and all other "isms", without relief. They are hungry for reality and truth, and it is time that they hear. God wants to use the members of His Kingdom to be a part of reaching the Asian nations for Jesus. The Kingdom of God is advancing!

Jesus provided the way to enter His kingdom, where He could be the King of ones life, community, and family.

Jesus came preaching the kingdom of God. *"The Kingdom of God,"* according to 1 Corinthians 4:20, *"does not consist in words, but in power."* Nor is the kingdom of God just of works; it is not just doing things in a religious fashion, but it is literally entering into the very power, the presence, and the glory of God, which He has given to us by the Holy Spirit who seals us unto redemption. The Kingdom of God is here, it is now, and it is amongst His worshipping community. Anyone who has truly sensed the presence of God, knows the reality that the Kingdom of God is within us.

The Entrance to the Kingdom

"Truly, truly, I say to you, unless one is born again, he cannot see the kingdom of God" (John 3:3).

"Truly, truly, I say to you, unless one is born of the water and the Spirit, he cannot enter the kingdom of God" (John 3:5)

It is through new birth that everyone called must enter the Kingdom. There is no other way. I remember when on staff of Youth For Christ a statement was often made "I know I am a Christian, because I was born into a Christian home or in a Christian nation." The standard response to this statement was "If I was born in a barn would that make me a cow, or if born in a garage would that make me a car, or if born in an oven, would that make me a biscuit!" The answer is obvious.

Birth is a violent act. Our precious mothers know, unless they were drugged, just how violent it is! The process of bringing life into the world from a biological perspective is most active, difficult and violent. The pain involved in the birthing process is a badge of courageous camaraderie that women everywhere share, a common bond that expresses their joy at participation in the production of glorious life.

The new birth into the kingdom of God has similar features. The condition of the un-regenerated life is fixed in darkness. By the preaching of the word of God one is called from a dark womb into the glorious light. When the call comes, and the step to emerge is imminent, one is forced or pressed into the new world. That is why, for most people, there are tears, not of joy but of sadness and remorse. There is a sense of guilt and shame. Being pushed from one world to the next is not easy, nor peaceful, as one is called and extracted from the old life and into a new one. Once established in the light, a new believer often feels somewhat strange, like stepping out of a dark room into a very bright one. It may be hard, both for the infant and for the spiritually reborn, to adjust to the light, to what they are seeing and experiencing. They have never been there before. They had been in a safe, warm, and comfortable place, and now they are thrust into a brand new environment. Yet it is a glorious one, filled with love, nurturing, warm milk, and wonderfully fascinating toys. God's plan is for all His children to grow, just as natural children do, to maturity, and eventually take one's full stature and place in the Kingdom of God, as functional self-sacrificing participants.

"The right king of monarchy is one where everybody goes about with the permanent conviction that the king can do no wrong."

- Chesterton

Chapter IV
More Kingdom Pictures

The Word of God speaks much about the Kingdom of God. In fact, the Kingdom is mentioned some 312 times in 299 verses throughout the Bible. The entire Old Testament contains pictures or types that illuminate the truths of the New Testament. We begin to understand principles for our spiritual life by reading and understanding what is said in the Old Covenant.

Let us discuss but a few of those Old and New Testament Kingdom scriptures, starting in 1 Samuel 3:13

> *And Samuel said to Saul, "You have acted foolishly; you have not kept the commandment of the LORD your God, which He commanded you, for now the LORD would have established your kingdom over Israel forever. But now your kingdom will not endure. The LORD had sought out for Himself a man after His own heart, and the LORD has appointed him as ruler over His people, because you have not kept what the LORD commanded you" (1 Samuel 13:13-14).*

Saul, Israel's first king, had been anointed by God through Samuel to be king in Israel. Head and shoulders above all others, he looked kingly. He looked and acted the part, but he was not the part in his heart. Aspects of his heart and character limited his ability to rule the way God intended.

So God said, *"you have acted foolishly. You have not kept the commandment of the Lord your God which He commanded you, for now the Lord would have established your kingdom over Israel forever."* Saul was unable to follow after God's heart because of fear of the people and disobedience. David was different; he had a heart faithfully in pursuit of God. And the heart is the heart of the matter!

We will find that the Old Testament contains many specific commandments of righteousness that we are also to follow in order to receive the fullness of what God intends for us.

Further, the Body of Christ is again being reminded of our responsibility to the Lord. Our first responsibility is to praise and worship Him. We are also responsible to one another in the body of Christ.

The sense of the fear of the Lord is beginning to return to the church. For some, this occurs through tragedies that happen, which are a clear result of absolute disobedience against God. In other cases, it is a hunger for a deeper relationship with the Lord, desiring to experience a greater sense of the presence of the Spirit. The church is giving up game-playing and self-righteousness nonsense, becoming serious about God and relationship with Him. That is wonderful! What God intended for Saul was to fulfill the plan and purpose of God through his life. He didn't hear the message. He did his own thing, without wisdom, ultimately costing him the kingdom.

"And David realized that the LORD had established him as king over Israel, and that He had exalted his kingdom for the sake of His people Israel." (2 Samuel 5:12)

God desires to establish, strengthen, and bless His people, but not just His people. He does not bless a person just for them. He blesses to establish the covenant. He blesses that one might be a blessing to others. What everyone has belongs to the Lord. He also blesses His people that they might share with others the blessings that He gives. David understood this, as demonstrated in spite his frequent ruthlessness and misguided passions, through his completion of the mission given him, of establishing God's throne in Israel. He moved God's people one step closer to fulfilling God's promise to Abraham, that all the nations of the world would be blessed through faith in God and His provision. Israel is "the church" in the Old Testament.

The Plan

The plan in David's heart was to establish the kingdom of God forever. That was also God's plan:

"He shall build a house for My name, and I will establish the throne of His kingdom forever" (2 Samuel 7:13).

Actually, the Kingdom of God began on earth before the time of Abraham. In fact, you can see God's plan for the kingdom in the life of the man and woman in the garden. From the very beginning, God's intention was for mankind to rule and reign over creation with God.

"Then God said, "Let us make man in Our image, according to Our likeness; and let them rule over the fish of the sea, and over the birds of the sky and over the cattle and over all the earth, and over every creeping thing that creeps on the earth." And God created man in His own image, in the image of God he created him; male and female He created them. And God blessed them, and God said to them "Be fruitful and multiply, and fill the earth and subdue it." (Gen. 1:26-28a)

All of history reveals God's unique and strategic dealings with His people, preparing His chosen to become vice-regents of His kingdom. Every week, believers pray, "Lord, Your Kingdom come," thinking in terms of the future because (it is assumed) that is when a Christian will find one's greatest fulfillment. When Jesus taught his disciples to pray the "Our Father", he was instructing them to pray for the day when the Kingdom Covenant would be transferred from National Israel to the Israel of God (the church), the transfer began on the day of Pentecost and continues to today. When Christ's Kingdom is finalized, the disciples of Christ will fulfill their destiny.

It is true when the consummation comes all believers will be transformed and placed in the position that God has pre-ordained, taking a position wrought by faithfulness to Christ. In other words, what one does here *does* determine where and how they will function in His ultimate Kingdom. As has been stated most aptly by George Ladd[1], The Kingdom of God is...but

---

[1] Attributed to Ladd from his work in *The Gospel of the Kingdom.*

is not yet fully. Christ inaugurated the kingdom via the cross and resurrection, but we will see it fully come (it is not delayed) when Christ returns for his bride. In the mean time, we (the church) are to occupy territory, by faith in Christ' triumph, planting churches everywhere until he comes. This is our ever present mandate.

From David to Solomon

"And Solomon sat on the throne of David, and his kingdom was firmly established."

God had promised David that He would establish his Kingdom eternally through David's son and descendants. The eternal Kingdom was established in Christ, but first a look at Solomon who was next after David's reign in Israel.

His Eternal Purpose

"Then I will establish the throne of your kingdom over Israel forever, just as I promised to your father David saying, 'You shall not lack a man on the throne of Israel.'" (I Kings 9:5)

God's plan has always been to establish His presence, His kingdom, here on the earth. In many ways the local church, as defined as the church in a locality, or city church (for more on this, see the author's book "Supernatural Architecture), is to be a place where the Kingdom of God is manifested and demonstrated. The church is to possess possessions for the Kingdom of God while here on this earth. All local churches, as part of the

Kingdom of God, are mystically linked with every other church around the world that claims Jesus Christ as Lord. All members are brothers and sisters regardless of the title hanging outside their door (or even if they have no door!). They, too, are actively seeking to *"possess their possessions,"* (Obadiah 17), to be a part of those who are actively seeking the expansion of the Kingdom of God.

God wants every local church that proclaims Jesus as Lord to possess the possessions that He has given! God may have given a pastor, for instance, a beautiful church building. It is up to the pastor and His people to possess and use this building for His glory. It is not to be used for anything else. It is to be a place where His Spirit is manifested, where everyone that walks through the door will experience the power of God (1 Cor. 14). That is His plan. However, it is not just for you (the local church and its' leadership) but for all brothers and sisters in Christ to benefit from in the locality.

> *"But He said to them, I must preach the Kingdom of God to other cities also; for I was sent for this purpose."* (Luke 4:43)

Jesus is saying, *"The purpose for which I came to the earth was to preach the Kingdom of God."* His ultimate aim was to establish His Kingdom forever in His own blood. This is why leaders everywhere are to speak the truth that God is establishing His Kingdom everywhere, and do all to propagate God's rule. God's rule is to be established over every aspect of life. He (Christ) is Lord and King, we are His loyal subjects, our highest good is to obey His commands and serve one another in love.

Luke 8:1 says,

> *"And it came about soon afterwards, that He began going about from one city and village to another, proclaiming and preaching the Kingdom of God and the twelve were with Him."*

Jesus never preached the church, though he proclaimed he would build it (Matt. 16:18); Paul never preached the church, though he travailed to see it matured. Part of Jesus purpose was to preach the Kingdom. He taught everyone who followed Him to do the same. That is why when the disciples stood to preach on the day of Pentecost, they simply preached about the Kingdom of God. "The Kingdom of God is here. How do we know it? Because Messiah has come. Jesus has come. He died on the cross according to the prophets, and He rose from the dead. He has established His Kingdom; it is here, it is now, and it is in us. And guess what? You can have His Kingdom too!" That is powerful! That is what Jesus preached, that is what the apostles preached, and that is what leaders are to preach as members of the Body of Christ today.

Luke 8:10 goes on to say,

> *"To you it has been granted to know the mysteries of the kingdom of God. But to the rest it is in parables; in order that seeing they may not see, and hearing they may not understand."*

Not everyone can understand the mysteries of the Kingdom. When the Bible is read in a public forum, some people will listen and say, "That is interesting literature." They have no idea what is being read because the

45

Kingdom of God is experienced spiritually. To them there is mystery, but to those who are believers, there is no mystery!

All Christians can have a clear understanding of the kingdom of God. It is simple: The King has come. He reigns over one's life, developing in His people a heart of a servant. The call as His chosen ones is to be his servant. When the King says, "Please get me a glass of water," that means, "Do it or die! Run as fast as you can, and don't you dare drop any on the way back!"

All of history reveals God's unique and strategic dealings with His people, preparing His chosen to become vice-regents of His kingdom.

But he is not a slave master. He is the King, and not just any King. Consider what he did for mankind! At what time in history did anyone else die for the world? Or took sin upon himself before Almighty God? All mankind deserved the guilt and the shame, but he took it! Praise His name!

An Illustration

King David was once in a battle close to his beloved Bethlehem. David's favorite sweet-water stream was close by, and he was overheard talking out loud to himself, "Ah, I am so thirsty! I would sure love a drink from that brook. Umm, my favorite fountain." Three warriors took off like bats. "The King wants it; we will do it for him!" They risked their lives to obtain the water. Of course, when David received the water, he could not drink it. He poured it out as a drink offering before the Lord because the men risked their own lives for his sake. Why?

Jesus never preached the church, though he proclaimed he would build it (Matt. 16:18).

They understood the Kingdom. The King deserves all the glory! He deserves all praise, devotion and servant-hood. Nothing He asks, and He usually asks through His leadership, should be too great a task. Why? Because, He saved us by His grace!

Another Picture

Luke 9:2 says, *"And He (Jesus) sent them out to proclaim the Kingdom of God and to perform healing."*

Showing God's power to the unsaved through the sign of healing is part of what the ministry is really about. Yes, God does heal in His Body, and yes, the gifts of the Holy Spirit are still available including the gift of healings for the body. But primarily, miraculous healings are a sign, a testimony that the Kingdom of God is here! That is the primary reason why miraculous healings are rarely seen in the local church, except at the beginning of its establishment. However, in its beginning, one will often see tremendous miraculous healings. This occurs to announce to a community that is without an adequate witness that the Kingdom of God has arrived. Thus, when a church is established in a community, they should expect the dynamic advertising of the King as the ministry of His word is preached under the anointing of the Holy Spirit.

The Kingdom Proclaimed Today

Preachers that have had the privilege of traveling to a two-thirds world nation have frequently seen the miraculous. Blind eyes are opened and the deaf and dumb speak. Not long ago I was in Pakistan. We had tremendous meetings with usually 5,000 to 6,000 people a night in attendance. Every night there were between 500 and 600 people saved. There were numbers of people, especially deaf and dumb children, who were absolutely and instantaneously delivered. They were running up and down the platform and talking, to the obvious delight of their parents and others under the tent. The Spirit of God was emphatically stating, "The Kingdom of God is here." The word preached was the same, "The Kingdom of God is here. Watch! God is going to bring His Kingdom in power." During Jesus' ministry He sent out His disciples to proclaim the Kingdom of God to places that had not heard the message before. They healed and delivered the demonized, and set at liberty the captives for the glory of God.

A Modern Version

Judith[2], a young lady in a Denver, Colorado, church, had been a part of our Bible College for some time. Shy by nature, she would sweat for weeks
before presenting a five-minute sermon. Her church had been experiencing a time of renewal and many had finally grasped what the kingdom of God is all about, including Judith. God began to work in her heart, and she asked the Lord for more boldness. It was not long before the Lord answered this prayer, one after God's own heart.

Judith received word that her father was going into the hospital for cancer surgery. She went to meet her parents at the hospital. Of course, she prayed all the way to the hospital, not knowing the gravity of the medical condition of her father. At the hospital, Judith and her parents were concerned about her father's surgery. They knew that if he died, he would go to be with the Lord; still, they were concerned and they comforted each other.

An elderly couple walked into the hospital. God spoke to Judith, "Go pray for that couple, and give them a word." This time, instead of succumbing to fear, she took an immediate step of bold faith. She had learned, "If I take a first step, fear stays behind me." So she began to move forward. She went to the unassuming couple and stated, "Hi! My name's Judith, and God just told me to pray for you. Do you mind if I pray?" "I don't care," was the reply. So she laid hands on this man and prayed for him. Judith

---

[2] The story is true, but names and circumstances have been altered for privacy sake.

was to find out later that this man had a most serious physical problem, and God came on him in power and healed him in the waiting room. In this situation, the man wasn't saved. In fact, he was a non-practicing Jew! I don't know if he became a believer or not. She simply announced, "The Kingdom of God is here!" She prayed for him, he was healed. She gave him a word about his life, his family, and about what God wanted to do in his life, and then she went back to her Dad. It was later that she fell apart, but with the couple she acted strong and natural. That is the way our natural life should be in the Kingdom.

Judith acted as Jesus taught His disciples to do. They learned: go out and proclaim the Kingdom of God. After teaching about the Kingdom, lay hands on the people. Cast out demons. Heal the sick. Proclaim liberty to spiritual captives. "As I have done, so you can do," said Jesus, "DO IT!" And as they did, God performed signs, wonders, and miracles. That's a part of our life in the Kingdom.

The New Covenant

In the New Testament, 1 Corinthians 15:50 says,

> *"Now I say this, brethren, that flesh and blood cannot inherit the Kingdom of God, nor does the perishable inherit the imperishable."*

The Kingdom of God is a spiritual Kingdom. Jesus is at the right hand of the Father. All believers are positionally and spiritually seated with Him in heavenly places (Ephesians 1:3). Yet the people of God are still very much a part of this physical realm. While the Kingdom is a spiritual one, it is also to manifest itself in the physical world, a merging with physical or natural. God wants to establish His Kingdom in the midst of the lived in world, and God intends to do it.

Taking a look at a few specific teachings about the Kingdom of God, found in the Gospels, can provide the New Covenant perspective. Matthew 3:2 reads,

"Repent, for the Kingdom of heaven is at hand."

Repentance is necessary for Kingdom living. Repentance is how we enter into the Kingdom, and it is how we continue to operate in the Kingdom. God expects every child of His to be continuously repentant, when the Holy Spirit reveals an area where change is needed. Repentance, forgiveness, and love should continuously flow out of our inner most beings. The natural Christian lifestyle should reveal the love and character of God, and repentance is required to keep His grace (favor) active and vibrant.

Some may think, "Repent? That means I have to have sinned in order to repent." What is meant is that, although there is a very good chance that one has not sinned -- today--there are still things about ones thinking that needs to change. The word repent comes from a root word meaning afterthought. It literally means, where one's thinking is in one direction, contrary to the word of God, it is to turn around and change direction. If a believer used to think carnally; now they think the way God thinks, according to His Word.

The Kingdom of God is a spiritual Kingdom.

If one is reading the Bible and praying every day, the Holy Spirit will speak almost daily about things that may need to change. God begins to change the perspectives and beliefs, as one confesses and truly repents in their heart before the Lord.

Because repentance means to change one's thinking, eventually even ones self-perception will change. Being an American, an Australian, an African or Asian will no longer matter, since embracing one's true nationality as a blood washed saint of the living God is most important. We are now Kingdom people. Truly, all Christians have a common blood, the blood of Jesus. Differences are no longer significant: "Well you know, that's the way my heritage is, my culture, the way I was trained...." Not any more. God is conforming the believers mind to the image of Christ through the revelation of God's Word being daily applied to one's life.

"And Jesus was going about in all Galilee, teaching in their synagogues and proclaiming the gospel of the Kingdom, and healing every kind of disease, and every kind of sickness among the people."

- Matthew 4:23

Chapter V
Matthew's View

It is in the Book of Matthew that Kingdom life and living are most notably proclaimed. Further, it is in the great teaching of the mountain (Sermon on the Mount), which we will refer to throughout this section, where Jesus' primary moral instruction for Kingdom living is found. A brief look at the Kingdom message in Matthew will shed greater light on this all important topic. Matthew 4:23 says,

> *"And Jesus was going about in all Galilee, teaching in their synagogues and proclaiming the gospel of the Kingdom, and healing every kind of disease, and every kind of sickness among the people."*

The preaching of the Kingdom of God was the primary ministry of Jesus. As He preached, the power of God was made available for healing and deliverance. His teaching ministry was different than most, filled with authority and the presence of God. Some brief comments will help us understand Jesus' thoughts. Matthew 5:3 and 10 states,

> *"Blessed are the poor in spirit for theirs is the Kingdom of Heaven. Blessed are those who have been persecuted for the sake of righteousness, for theirs is the kingdom of heaven."*

It's not "blessed are the poor." but, "the poor in spirit," or those who are meek and humble before the Lord, "for theirs is the Kingdom of Heaven."

(The Kingdom of Heaven and the Kingdom of God are spoken of synonymously.) For those who mourn especially over their own sinful condition, God provides comfort; through Christ's provision the meek or gentle will inherit the earth. That is, through the quiet strength of faithful perseverance we will see Satan and his purposes destroyed (See Rom. 16:20).

Righteousness is imparted to us through Christ righteous act. Yet, we are to continue to hunger and thirst for his righteousness (right thinking and right behavior) to be manifested in our daily walk. As we will see later, righteousness is a key component of kingdom living.

To receive mercy we must forgo judgmentalism in favor of mercy to others. Men and women living vibrantly in the kingdom of God have given up the right to judge to the Lord, and have acknowledged their need for mercy by being grace oriented to others.

A pure heart is one which has been cleaned by the blood of Christ. His promise to all believers is that we will indeed see him; a precious promise of the kingdom.

Peacemakers seek unity over diversity, believers who suffer persecution for right living have truly possessed the kingdom of God in their hearts.

The character of God manifested in people demonstrates the kingdom is present. Thank God his kingdom has and will come to all his children.

Those who are willing to humble themselves under the mighty hand of God, will be exalted, but if we constantly attempt to convince God of our brilliance, we will have numerous difficulties. We don't know all the answers! I have had wonderful times of fellowship with local pastors, but we all ask, "God, what is the answer for our city?" We preach, teach, and do outreaches. Our purpose is to reach people for Jesus, to disciple them to maturity so they can fulfill their destiny. "Our hearts, Lord, are right before You. Where is the breakthrough? What has to happen, Lord, to see your kingdom in power?" Only the Lord knows! Jesus prays for your city every day. The Holy Spirit is also interceding. The answers are there. We have not tapped into them yet, but we will in time and season. Yet, on the other hand, every time an individual professes Christ, or an injustice is made right, the Kingdom is manifested in our seeing.

Even horrendous incidents, like the bombing tragedy of Oklahoma City or the terrorist attack on New York City and the Pentagon can be used to bring our focus onto God.

God will reveal to us what His purpose is, and may use differing circumstances to achieve his purposes. Even horrendous incidents, like the bombing tragedy of Oklahoma City or the terrorist attack on New York City and the Pentagon can be used to bring our focus onto God. Although these were terrible tragedies caused by wicked and deceived men, many are finding comfort in the local church in the aftermath of these incidents.

In spite of circumstances horrific and painful, we are to continue to proclaim His Kingdom until our breakthrough comes, in whatever way God allows it to occur.

> *"Blessed are those who have been persecuted for the sake of righteousness, for theirs is the Kingdom of Heaven" "Whoever then annuls one of the least of these commandments and so teaches others, shall be called least in the Kingdom of Heaven. But whoever keeps and teaches them; he shall be called great in the Kingdom of Heaven." (Matthew 5:10, 19).*

Jesus gave a synopsis of the entire Law to His disciples:

> *"'YOU SHALL LOVE THE LORD YOUR GOD WITH ALL YOUR HEART, AND WITH ALL YOUR SOUL, AND WITH ALL YOUR MIND.'*
> *This is the great and foremost commandment.*
> *The second is like it, 'YOU SHALL LOVE YOUR NEIGHBOR AS YOURSELF.'*
> *On these two commandments depend the whole Law and the Prophets (Matthew 22:37-40).*

These are the commandments to which Jesus referred. If you will love the Lord your God with your heart, soul, mind, and strength, and your neighbor as yourself, you will fulfill the whole law. If you will also teach others to do the same, you will be seen as great in the Kingdom. Does that sound impossible? It is not, yet it is so difficult for most Christians! "I'm to love you, Lord, with all of my heart, all of my soul, all of my might, everything that's within me, but am I to love that awful neighbor of mine? Lord, You know him! Not even You could possibly love him! Could You?"

"And love my neighbor as myself."

Maybe you do not love yourself. "Well, I'm not supposed to love myself! I'm to crucify myself." Have you ever tried to nail yourself to a cross? You can nail one arm, but what do you do with the other one? Unless you have a long hammer and a very strong jaw, it cannot be done! That is the work of the Holy Spirit as you submit yourself to the Lord. He deals with the issues of the flesh. We must keep the commandments to the best of our abilities if the Kingdom of God is to be manifested in our lives. That means wholeheartedly loving God, loving our neighbors as we love ourselves, which flows from a new creation image or a godly self-image.

Who are you in Christ? Are you a worm? Of course not, that is an Old Testament concept that no longer applies (and did not in Jesus' day). We are the righteousness of God in Christ, new creations; adopted children! We are inheritors of the glory of God! Would you look at your child, and say, "Oh, what a mistake! You are worthless! I hope you wouldn't do that to your children! God doesn't do that to us. He looks at us with love; we're the apple of His eye. So we can love our neighbors as we love ourselves. Having godly self-respect, we should also show godly respect to our neighbors. And who are our neighbors? Everybody.

Parables for Today

Let us look at a few more analogies of the Kingdom of Heaven, found in Matthew 13:

"The Kingdom of Heaven may be compared to a man who sowed good seed in his field. The Kingdom of Heaven is like a mustard seed, which a man took and sowed in his field. The Kingdom of Heaven is like leaven, which a woman took and hid in three pecks of meal until it was all leavened. The Kingdom of Heaven is like a treasure hid in the field, which a man found and hid, and from joy over it he went and sold all that he had and bought that field. The Kingdom of Heaven is like a merchant seeking fine pearls. The Kingdom of Heaven is like a dragnet cast into the sea gathering fish of every kind."

Jesus described the Kingdom of God in pictorial language. He described it as a seed of the mustard plant, but any kind of seed will do. A seed does not produce one for one. Each seed produces a very large quantity in comparison to itself. That seed must fall to the ground and die before it can bring forth fruit. **The Kingdom of God, once planted in soil (the heart), will produce fruit.**

Every believer should produce fruit. The fruit of the Kingdom is the fruit of character; love, joy, peace, etc. (Gal. 5:22, 23). Fruitful living will bring others into the Kingdom of God. God intends for us to be fruitful. If we are not, we have somehow suffocated or squelched the natural growth producing, vibrant process of the Kingdom of God that has been placed in us. He didn't create us in the natural or in the spiritual realm to be fruitless, but to be extremely fruitful to bring forth yields up to one hundredfold. The Kingdom is constantly expanding.

You may not notice it at first; a seed looks so small, nothing to it. "What do you mean, confess with your mouth, believe with your heart, I mean, big deal...." But once you do confess with your mouth and believe in your heart, something is planted in your spirit. God's Spirit and His Word begins to grow, and expand, expand, and expand, until you cannot contain it. You are not supposed to contain it. We are meant to open our heart and mouth, and proclaim that which God has planted in our heart to the world.

The Kingdom is like leaven. Leaven takes over everything. It starts with a little amount, just a little bit of yeast. But after a while, the **Kingdom (yeast) grows to permeate every aspect of our lives**. Our thinking, speech, and action reflect Kingdom principles. Our focus of life will be a Kingdom focus. "Yes, Lord, what would You have me to do this day? Every day will be focused on living your life as a member of the Kingdom, just as leaven permeates a loaf of bread.

The Kingdom is like a pearl, or the treasure hidden in a field. There are many people searching for gold on the island of Mindanao, Philippines, even though rumors of gold are a scam. But if someone gave you a treasure map and said, "There is a gold treasure absolutely guaranteed to be on the island of Mindanao!" What would you do to get it? What would you do if you knew that a whole shipload of gold waited to be discovered which would enrich you beyond your imagination? If you had to sell your car to buy the ticket and to purchase your gear, if you had to beg, borrow, or nearly steal to get there, would you not do it? The Kingdom is so priceless, that once people understand, they yield to God. "You mean God in Christ, Christ in me, the hope of glory? Really? For me? How much?" "It's free." "C'mon, HOW MUCH? I'll pay anything for it!" Those that embrace the Kingdom of God like that become servants of God. **Those that understand how precious the Kingdom is, sell all.** With great joy they're willing to give up anything to see the kingdom of God established in their heart, family and their community.

The Kingdom is like a dragnet. You cast that net into the sea and expect to bring in fish of all kind. Whosoever, all races, creeds and colors, are invited into the Kingdom. Glory to God. **God is always expanding His Kingdom, and as kingdom people are work with the Holy Spirit and God's leadership to see his ever expanding Kingdom grow.**

"Righteousness as exemplified by Christ is not merely the absence of vice or the presence of virtue. It is a consuming passion for God which sends you forth in His name to establish His kingdom."

- Irving Peake Johnson

Chapter VI
Character of the Kingdom:
Righteousness

Righteousness, peace, and joy characterize God's Kingdom. *For the kingdom of God is. . .righteousness and peace and joy in the Holy Spirit"* (Rom. 14:16-17).

The Kingdom of God is not eating and drinking, materialism, or our own personal comfort. It is not building our own empires. Our own prosperity does not mean we are furthering God's Kingdom. Only by using our prosperity for the establishment of His Covenant do we demonstrate the Kingdom of God in our hearts. The things of the Kingdom are otherwise: righteousness, peace and joy in the Holy Spirit.

First and most important is righteousness. Without righteousness there will be no peace or joy. Thank God, He has made us righteous in Christ, because of the blood of His Son.

The Apostle Paul was near the end of his life when he was writing to the Church in Rome. During his early days, he was been an incredible man, on-fire, zealous, out to conquer the world. However, at the end of his journey, he was relatively confined. This no doubt gave him cause to think, "What is the most important thing that I could impart to the people to whom I have had the privilege of ministering? *Righteousness!"*

Righteousness means right moral relationships with God, with oneself, with man, and with nature or creation. Right moral relationships involve living according to God's commandments. We are to treat our neighbors and ourselves with love and respect. We are not to abuse our bodies or our minds. We are to live righteously.

Only by using our prosperity for the establishment of His Covenant do we demonstrate the Kingdom of God in our hearts.

The world would not be in such an environmental mess if mankind was in proper relationship with God's creation. God commissioned mankind to manage the earth and improve it, if that were possible. Instead, we have misused the earth and its resources, produced irreparable pollution, and we are all suffering for it. That was never God's plan. For example, there is an unbelievable level of air and water pollution in Manila, Philippines. If you were to visit Metro Manila you would see hideous destruction of the environment. That is just one city. Mexico City is much worse. All aspects of our life needs to be in proper relationship, including a healthy relationship with the world God created for us.

The word moral has to do with God's morality. Our relationships should be based upon what God says. Standards of morality have been established in His word, such as the Ten Commandments, the Beautitudes, etc., that let us know how we are to live. These standards are not the morality of our culture, of course. If we governed our lives according to current cultural mores, we could do basically whatever we wanted, eat drink and be merry, for tomorrow we can do it again!

One observation I have made in my many travels is that anywhere Catholicism reigns or has a strong influence, immorality follows. For example, in many nations with strong histories of religious domination there is a high degree of sexual immorality. That means there is an acceptance of incest, child abuse, rape, homosexuality, and more, in these countries. I have heard believers (sadly, even leaders) in some cultures say, "But you don't understand, Brother Stan. That's just the way we are. That's our culture." Culture must be measured against the Word of God! Where culture conflicts with God's Word, we must bow to Scripture and deny culture.

On the great African continent, tribalism and lust for power is prevalent even in the Church. Leaders there will state, "This is our way! We do not want the white man's way." I certainly agree that European ways are as dysfunctional as any other. However, our true identity is to be found in Christ and His Word, and our culture must conform to the Kingdom if we are to positively affect our world for Christ.

In looking at this word righteousness, there are several important components that we should note.

Righteousness comes to us through redemption.

> *"In Him we have our redemption through His blood, the forgiveness of our trespasses, according to the riches of His grace"* (Ephesians 1:7).

We receive it by the impartation of the Holy Spirit at our new birth. We have been redeemed from death by the wonderful blood of Jesus. Of course, **His righteousness is reckoned to us by faith.**

> *"Then (Abraham) believed in the Lord, and He reckoned it to him as righteousness"* (Genesis 15:6).

> *"For in it the righteousness of God is revealed from faith to faith; as it is written, 'BUT THE RIGHTEOUS man SHALL LIVE BY FAITH'"* (Romans 1:17).

We receive it when we accept Christ as Savior and Lord by faith. Without faith it is impossible to please God. And without faith it is impossible to live fully in the Kingdom of God. Our life is to be filled with faith and faithfulness.

Righteousness must be received.

> *"Blessed is a man who perseveres under trial; for once he has been approved, he will receive the crown of life, which the Lord has promised to those who love Him"* (James 1:12).

In other words, although the message of the Kingdom of God is constantly going forth, until an unbeliever believes and says, "I do," it does not actually manifest. One must receive the provision that God has made through Christ. It is equally true that as believers we receive His righteousness daily and are to apply it to our lives judiciously. This does not refer to getting re-saved. We are saved, and we are being saved, and we will be saved. We are saved at the time that we ask Christ into our lives. But we also need to be sanctified; becoming pure and separate from sin. Sanctification is a part of our salvation. We are being saved, and we will be saved, or glorified, at the end of our natural life or at the end of the age. Applying His righteousness and His principles from God's word to our lives is a daily part of life and walk in the Kingdom of God.

Righteousness is given to us as a rescue.

> *"The Lord knows how to rescue the godly from temptation, and to keep the unrighteous under punishment for the day of judgment"* (2 Peter 2:9).

We have been rescued from sin and ourselves. What joy this should bring to every believer's heart. Who knows where any of us would be if Jesus had not rescued us. Thank God for His rescue! God rescues and restores us to the fullness of what He intended for us. This is both a marvelous event and an ongoing process.

We are wrapped in righteousness.

*"I will rejoice greatly in the LORD, my soul will exult in my God;
for He has clothed me with garments of salvation, He has **wrapped
me with a robe of righteousness**"* (Isaiah 61:10).

We actually wear a robe of righteousness that has been given to us. Let us
walk as though everyone could see it! A robe of righteousness would
indicate to all around that I am a member of the Kingdom of God. The
book of Revelation talks of a robe of white, beautiful, glorious, and
glimmering, that all the saints of God wear. It is not just future that we
receive the robe of righteousness, but we have it now, in Christ, and we
are to daily walk in that righteousness.

We are saved, and we are being saved, and we will be saved.

To help us walk the way God wants us to in the Kingdom we must reckon
ourselves dead to the old life, and receive again our righteousness through
that daily reckoning. Daily we must remember we are alive in Christ, thus
we affirm afresh God's reign over us. How do we do that? We do it
through prayer. "Lord, I thank You that my old self is dead! I thank You
Lord, that when You died on the cross, I died with you. When You were
buried, Lord I was buried with you. When You rose again, Lord, I rose
with you. Right now, I am seated in the Heavenlies with You. Thank You,
Lord! Today, Lord I am robed in Your righteousness, I am filled with the
Spirit and I consider my old self as dead; I am alive in Christ!

Are you asking, "Did that prayer use the present tense, 'I am?'" Yes! God's name is "I AM THAT I AM." We are not God, of course, but we are in Christ. It is Christ in us which is the hope of glory; we have a part of the glory of God in us. We can say, "I am, because He is." And when we are saying, "I am," we are identifying with I AM THAT I AM. We are affirming that, "Your nature is in me. Your glory is in me. You placed it there. I did not deserve it but it is there, and I'm forever grateful!"

We must identify with having that robe of righteousness every morning when we awake. We can look in the mirror and say, "Hey! Glory to God, you're a man of God. You're a man of faith and power. It does not matter if I feel like it, for I know who I am in Christ!" It is important to spiritually brush off your robe in the morning. Remember to walk in His righteousness through the day because of who you are in Christ.

Because of Christ, **righteousness is restored to us.**

> *"Then he will pray to God, and He will accept him, that he may see His face with joy. And He may restore His righteousness to man"*
> (Job 33:26).

Thank God that our righteousness, stolen by Satan in the Garden, has been restored to us by Christ's death on the Cross.

We know that God is the judge of this world. Eventually we will also judge the nations with Christ. We need to learn now the judgment of God.

How good to learn to evaluate things properly and to make judgments according to righteousness (Ps. 9:8).

"For the righteous LORD loves righteousness" (Ps. 11:7).

When God sees us doing something right, God rejoices. Do you want to give the Lord joy? Live righteously, meaning, don't just think right, but do right as well. When children do their chores without whining, moaning, or complaining; if they work to the best of their ability, that pleases the Lord not to mention their parents. When we keep commitments, we act rightly, it pleases the Lord. When we don't, of course, it does disappoint Him, because we are operating at a lesser standard than what we can in God.

Remember, righteousness is not something that flows naturally from us. We couch potato men would just as soon lounge on the couch as get up and help with the dishes, clean around the house, or help take care of diapers (or nappies). We tell our wives that diapers are not our gift. But it is nobody's gift. It's just a gift that keeps on giving, and somebody's got to take care of it! When we act right, in righteousness, God is pleased, but it is something we must work at (Ps. 15:2).

When we have come clean with any issue of sin and are thus living right before the Lord, our orientation (face) becomes towards God. Most of us love to look into the face of the Lord through His word. There is nothing more exhilarating than to wake up in the morning, with the knowledge that we are clean. It is easy to come to the Lord at times like that. But when we have sinned, and we know it, and have not properly faced it, it is difficult approaching the Lord. We know what we should do, but to do what is right takes courage (Ps. 17:15).

We know if we confess, He will forgive us. Human nature is such, however, that we sometimes avoid even the thing that we need the most. Yet, even as with the man and woman in the garden when we sin, God comes to us, not to condemn, but to offer his righteousness to us once again.

> *"Therefore has the LORD recompensed me according to my righteousness, according to the cleanness of my hands in His sight"* (Ps. 18:24).

Though this is an Old Covenant passage, but there are certain blessings that come to us through the process of sowing and reaping. When we sow righteousness, we will reap righteousness. When we sow destruction, we will reap destruction. The Word is saying that we will be rewarded according to our right living.

We may not see the recompense immediately. Many times we may be living right, doing right, even tithing and giving offerings. Yet we struggle, and wonder why. There is a time for sowing, and a time for reaping. There is a time and season for everything. Remain faithful, and you will see the reaping. God has promised.

> *"He restores my soul, He leads me in the paths of righteousness, for His name's sake"* (Ps. 23:3).

Righteousness is not hard to find, God wants to lead us there! He has a path for us to walk. If we will simply submit ourselves to the Lord, he will lead us.

It is not as though we have to stretch, work, fight and scream to find that path. It is simple. Just follow the Lord through obeying God's word.

> *"In Thee O LORD do I put my trust. Let me never be ashamed. Deliver me in They righteousness"* (Ps. 31:1).

Even our deliverance will come as we simply live right. Many people are hung up on their problems. But as they begin to live right according to the Word of God, many of their struggles, one by one, fall away on their own. Most behaviors do not need personal deliverance; just live right, and most of our problems will take care of themselves (Ps. 31:1).

> *"You love righteousness and hate wickedness; therefore God, Thy God, has anointed you with the oil of gladness above your fellows"* (In Ps. 45:7).

There is a linkage between righteousness, peace, and joy. Many scriptures speak about these characteristics of the Kingdom of God in tandem. The fact is, without living right before God (not perfect, but moving towards maturity) we have no peace. For example, if a husband and wife have an argument, where one party was more wrong than the other, forgiveness must be sought, given and granted, restoring the communication in the relationship. Right standing (relational harmony) must be restored before peace (let alone joy) will return to a house. Thus, righteousness is the foundation for peace, and peace (tranquil mind) sets the stage for joy.

"As righteousness tends to life, so he that pursues evil, it is to his own death" (Prov. 11:19).

Righteousness leads us toward life. It is our responsibility as adults to teach right and wrong to young people. Many youth experience temptations and strong peer pressure without a firm understanding of right from wrong. In reality, a majority of parents assume that their children know right from wrong, because they may not have had problems managing them when they were young. A child may cooperate because of the fear of punishment, or they may be temperamentally compliant. This does not guarantee that they really know what right living is all about.

Other parents assume that their children will learn right and wrong in Sunday School. I hate to disillusion you, but the allotted time each week for instruction is insufficient for teaching them righteousness or God's ways. It is not unusual for a young person to reach the teenage years, with a very limited understanding of the expectations of God. We must take every opportunity as a parent to lay down principles of truth for teens. It may deliver them from much heartache (along with the parents!).

As much as possible, let us sow the seeds of righteousness by teaching and training children what righteousness is when they're very young. Then when they are older, they will be able to make decisions based upon a positive understanding of what God requires, instead of upon how much one can get away with, with peers or parents (Prov. 12:28).

"Righteousness exalts a nation, but sin is a reproach to any people" (Prov. 14:34).

When you hear this, think about your government leaders. Pray for their salvation! Some of our (the United States) former leaders were interesting fellows, with interesting backgrounds, but not exactly paragons of virtue. The behavior of a leader can affect the nation as a whole, both in the negative and the positive. Righteousness exalts a nation; it lifts it up. The opposite, sin, is a reproach to any people. We shouldn't look at the sin that is rampant within our government, wink at it and say, "Oh well, there is nothing we can do." No, let us pray that righteous leaders will be raised up who will be able to govern in a godly fashion.

Ultimately, we are looking for a city of righteousness. When Jesus returns for His Church, His Bride, He will set up His ultimate Kingdom. It will be a Kingdom filled with righteousness.

One of our titles as believers is *"Righteous Ones."*

"Now he that ministers seed to the sower both minister bread for your food, and multiply your seed sown, and increase the fruits of your righteousness" (2 Cor. 9:10).

Righteousness can increase. There are certain people who, by their very presence bring you closer to the Lord. You almost sense God's presence when you are with them. Cherish and nurture such relationships; eventually we become like those we affiliate with! When you are around some people, you sense the righteousness of God. You know that they have a close and intimate relationship with the Lord. Their righteousness has increased, and so can yours.

Heb. 12:11 talks about discipline:

> *"Now no chastening (or discipline) for the present seems to be joyous, but grievous. Nevertheless, afterwards it yields the peaceable fruit of righteousness to them which are exercised thereby."*

> *"And the fruit of righteousness is sown in peace of them that make peace"* (James 3:18).

Righteousness. God wants us to live right, have right thinking that leads to right behavior before our fellow man. Right thinking is a function of daily interaction with God's word, and applying what we learn judiciously and faithfully to our daily walk. Righteousness is a characteristic of every true believer, and a characteristic of those walking and working in the glorious kingdom of God.

"Peace, like every other rare and precious thing, doesn't come to you. You have to go and get it."

- Faith Forsyte

"Peace is not the absence of conflict from life, but the ability to cope with it."

- Sun Dial

"Blessed are the peacemakers."

- Matthew 5:9

Chapter VII
Character of the Kingdom:
Peace

Peace is defined as calmness, or tranquility. The entire world is looking for peace. I was in a jet on the way to the Philippines, reading an article on Jimmy Carter and the Carter Center in Atlanta, Georgia. His focus now, as a former United States President, is to be a peacemaker. He travels from nation to nation where there has been conflict, trying to negotiate peace. That is wonderful, even admirable. We wish great success for him, but we know according to the Word of God, that there will be no ultimate world peace, until Christ's kingdom is fully manifested in the earth. Though world peace may not be achieved outside of Christ's return, we can have peace in our hearts in the midst of troubled waters, and can walk in peace, making it an integral part of our life as members of the Kingdom of God. So what is peace and how can we experience it this side of glory?

Isa. 9:6 describes Jesus as ***"the Prince of Peace."*** Provided here is a picture of the precious peace that has been purchased for us by the Prince of Peace, Christ Jesus! He comes as would a Prince to all of us, and offers to us His peace. Jesus said during His earthly ministry,

> *"Peace I leave with you, My peace I give to you: not as the world gives, give I unto you. Let not your heart be troubled, neither let it be afraid"* (John 14:27).

This is not always easy to receive, but nonetheless, God wants us to live our life filled with His peace, even in the midst of life's troubles.

According to Eph. 2:6, **our peace comes through our position in Christ.** He

> *"has raised us up together, and made us sit together in heavenly places in Christ Jesus."*

What is our position now? We're seated in the Heavenlies, with Christ. We are far above every principality and power. That does not mean we are so heavenly minded that we are of no earthly good. It means we recognize a higher level of authority in our life than what the world offers. We recognize and submit to a greater higher power than that to which many in Alcoholics Anonymous do (that whatever you believe in is fine). Jesus is our Higher Power, our Prince, our Lord, our King.

There will be no ultimate world peace, until Christ's kingdom is fully manifested in the earth.

He has invited us to His level, glory to God, through the blood of Jesus. We have a new position that makes us almost invincible. That does not mean we never experience trials and tribulations. We will. But in the middle of them, if we will remind ourselves of our position in Christ, we can experience and enjoy the peace that comes with that position.

Our peace comes through pardon.

> *"Let the wicked forsake his way, and the unrighteous man his thoughts: and let him return unto the LORD, and he will have mercy upon him; and to our God, for he will abundantly pardon"* (Isa. 55:7).

Think of what you have been forgiven of! Is it not wonderful? You can probably name off many things, and laugh. It is covered; it is under the blood! It is gone, and God does not even remember it! If the devil reminds me of something that God has forgotten, do I need to pay attention to it? If some would-be prophet reminds me of something God has forgotten, I know he is listening to a familiar spirit rather than to the Holy Spirit. Because of Jesus' pardon, we have His peace.

Peace comes through possession.

> *And having made peace through the blood of His cross, by Him to reconcile all things unto Himself"* (Col. 1:20).

We must possess our peace, but also Christ is our possession. He is in us. Christ in us is the hope of Glory (Col. 1:27).

We must lean not to dwell on the past. When we think about the present and our future, we are excited. Hallelujah! We do not know what or how, exactly, but we do know His plans for us are good. That is a wonderful blessing. He gives us peace.

Peace comes because we live in His presence. Psalm 23 pictures a life lived in God's presence.

> *"He leads us beside still waters."*

In His presence we have His peace. David found peace in God's creation, and so can we. Thus, we need to stop and smell the roses once in a while, relax in God's provision.

> *"Cease striving and know the presence of God"* (Isa. 46:10).

What a wonderful picture. He leads us to where the water is fresh and restorative. Regardless the external turmoil, as we mediate (a key) on His word, picturing the peace of the riverside, we possess the peace, incorporating it into our hearts and minds. Peace is something that is desperately needed in the Body of Christ. We will not have peace as long as we live less than righteously before the Lord. We might be able to assuage our guilt or use denial effectively to avoid facing the truth, but we will not really know God's deep peace. That comes only when you know you are living right with God. Are you doing everything He has asked you to do?

Let us review a few more verses about peace.

> *"I will both lay me down in peace, and sleep: for Thou, LORD, only makes me dwell in safety."* (Ps 4:8).

Sometimes I have to remind myself that God's plan is for me to be safe! I was at Brother Eddie Villanueva's compound in the middle of the Philippines, when they received a bomb threat. They asked me what I wanted to do. I said, "I'm tired. I'm going to bed!"

God had promised me safety. I know what my commission is and I also have a prophetic promise from the Lord that says I will not die until I have fulfilled what God has called me to do. I have a lot of work to do, Glory to God! It gives me a sense of peace.

Prophetic insight, by the way, will always give you peace. When you have heard the voice of God, when you have heard someone say God has great plans for your future, what does that tell you? It tells you there is a future! That should give you a sense of peace, no matter what anyone else says.

> *"The LORD will give strength unto His people, the LORD will bless His people with peace"* (Ps. 29:11).

He wants to bless us with peace.

> *"Depart from evil and do good; seek peace, and pursue it"* (Ps. 34:14).

Sometimes peace must be pursued. In the pursuit of peace, we must sometimes run from one who would steal our peace or tear us to pieces. Sometimes we need to lock our doors, unplug our telephones, and avoid people that effectively rob us of our peace. Gossips, and there seem to be a lot of them, can ruin our peace.

Many people do not consider another's needs. All they care about is their own situation. I do not refer to someone in genuine crisis. People in distress do need help, but not necessarily your immediate attention.

If you live with someone who wants to constantly argue, battle, and rebel, your peace will vanish. What should you do? Pursue peace.

Sometimes you have to make decisions about your relationships. Set boundaries, so that your life remains peaceful. When in a time of prayer, turn off your phone, so no one bothers you. Thus, God, who can intervene any time He wants, can speak to your heart at peace. Clients in my counseling practice have had crises at different times. But, I have told them they can have a crisis when ever they like, except during my quiet time or on the weekends! You can set boundaries in order to keep your place of peace. Pursue it, which literally means, fight for it. It is a part of our inheritance from God.

> *"But the meek shall inherit the earth, and shall delight themselves in the abundance of peace"* (Ps. 37:11).

Meekness and peace seem to walk hand in hand. Moses was called the meekest man who ever lived on earth. Jesus was also meek and mild. Jesus said,

> *"Blessed are the meek"* (Mat. 5:5).

God wants us to walk in meekness. With it will come peace. Meekness is not weakness, but quiet strength, confidence in who we are in Christ.

> *"Mark the perfect (or righteous) man, and behold the upright, for the end of that man is peace"* (Ps. 37:37).

We become like those with whom we affiliate. As we observe those living right with God, we will observe peace in the midst of storms.

> *"Mercy and truth are met together, righteousness and peace have kissed each other"* (Ps. 85:10).

They work hand in hand as part of our life in the Kingdom.

> *"Great peace have they which love your law, and nothing shall offend them"* (Ps. 119:165).

People easily offended are generally not people of the Word. Knowing a number of Scriptures does not make one a person of the Word. In other words, the Word may be tucked into their brains but not hidden in their hearts. They don't live according to the Word. If they did, they would live in peace. When someone slights them, they might say, "Well, you know, everybody has a bad day every once in a while. Lord, bless them, give them a good day, Lord, so that the next time I see them, we'll have a wonderful interaction together!" Without the Word they may think instead, "That's it! I'm *never* coming back to this church again! It's full of hypocrites! And they're all ANGRY! Except for me, of course!"

> *"Pray for the peace of Jerusalem. They shall prosper that love You"* (Ps. 122:6).

I believe that is still a commandment today. We need to pray for the peace of Jerusalem, both for the Jerusalem which is in Israel, and for the Jerusalem which is the Church.

> *"He that is void of wisdom despiseth his neighbor; but a man of understanding hold his peace"* (Prov. 11:12)

A man of understanding knows when to shut up!

> *"Deceit is in the heart of them that imagine evil, but to the counselors of peace is joy"* (Prov. 12:20).

We see the linkage of Righteousness, peace and joy again. Peace comes from righteousness. And when we are living in peace, it creates the atmosphere whereby joy can emerge.

> *"When a man's ways please the LORD, He makes even his enemies to be at peace with him"* (Prov. 16:7).

> *"A time to love, a time to hate; a time of war, a time of peace"* (Eccl. 3:8).

God knows it is time for peace. If you have been experiencing real struggles, ask God for His peace.

Isaiah 53:5 says,

> *"But He was wounded for our transgressions, He was bruised for our iniquities; the chastisement of our peace was upon Him, and with His stripes we are healed."*

We receive peace because Jesus became our peace offering, satisfying God's wrath.

> *"And as they thus spoke, Jesus Himself stood in the middle of them and said unto them, Peace be unto you"* (Luke 24:36).

The disciples were often caught in traumatic situations. Once they were fighting to stay afloat on the sea of Galilee, huge waves buffeting their boat. Jesus walked out to them in the midst of the storm, looking rather spooky. To the disciples He said, "Fear not!", and to the waves, "Peace! Be still." He had the ability to speak a word of peace. We also have the ability in God to speak a word of peace. God has given to us the ability to speak peace in the most difficult situation. Sometimes that word has to be hard and firm. Sometimes it is soft. *"A soft answer turns away wrath"* (Prov. 15:1).

God gives us the ability to speak a word of peace.

"Peace I leave with you, My peace I give unto you, not as the world gives, give I unto you. Let not your heart be troubled, neither let it be afraid" (John 14:27).

"These things I have spoken unto you, that in Me ye might have peace. In the world you will have tribulation, but be of good cheer; I have overcome the world" (John 16:33).

"Be of "hilarious laughter!" Laugh, enjoy, have fun, play! It can bring us to greater peace in the midst of any kind of storm." – Source Unknown

"Real joy comes not from ease or riches or from praise of men, but from doing something worthwhile."

-   Sir Wilfred Grenfell

"Weeping may endure for a night, but joy comes in the morning."

- Psalms 30:5

Chapter VIII
The Character of the Kingdom:
Joy

Joy; the word means delight. If you won the lottery, you'd be delighted. (Not that any Christians play the Lotto!) You were no doubt delighted when you first fell in love. The experience of joy was doubtless overwhelming bliss.

In a similar fashion, Jesus is our joy. Several key scriptures speak of this wonderful joy, and of their importance to us.

John 15:7-11 says,

> "If you abide in Me, and My words abide in you, ask whatever you wish, and it shall be done for you. "By this is My Father glorified, that you bear much fruit, and so prove to be My disciples. "Just as the Father has loved Me, I have also loved you; abide in My love. "If you keep My commandments, you will abide in My love; just as I have kept My Father's commandments, and abide in His love. "These things I have spoken to you, that My joy may be in you, and that your joy may be made full.

John 17:13, 21 says,

> "But now I come to Thee; and these things I speak in the world, that they may have My joy made full in themselves. ...that they may all be one; even as Thou, Father, art in Me, and I in Thee, that they also may be in Us; that the world may believe that Thou didst send Me.

I John 1:1-4 says,

> What was from the beginning, what we have heard, what we have seen with our eyes, what we beheld and our hands handled, concerning the Word of Life and the life was manifested, and we have seen and bear witness and proclaim to you the eternal life, which was with the Father and was manifested to us what we have seen and heard we proclaim to you also, that you also may have fellowship with us; and indeed our fellowship is with the Father, and with His Son Jesus Christ. And these things we write, so that our joy may be made complete.

One of the desires of Jesus' heart, and of the Apostle John's, was that our joy might be made complete, or full. The way our joy is made complete is through our intimate fellowship (Koinonia) with Jesus. Jesus walked in His daily life filled with joy. Why? Because He had an intimate relationship with His Father. I don't know what He saw when He gazed into heaven, but he often stated, "I only do what I see my Father do." He had excellent spiritual vision. He was able to see things in the prophetic 'now.' He must have seen as presently true His prayer,

> *"I want them to be one, Father, as you and I are one, that our joy may be in them"* (John 17:21, paraphrased).

What would cause such joy, such delight, as He looked on His Father? The picture I have is similar to the one that I love to see when a young child first sees his Dad come home from work. A little child is still enchanted with dad thinking his Dad walks on water, never doing anything wrong. When Dad first comes home, the child throws off restraint, runs and jumps in Daddy's arms! There might follow a mutual hug-and-kiss fest, playing together, and roughhousing. There is a sense of delight! There is joy. I can only surmise the joy Jesus' felt knowing he was doing the Father's will, that He was pleasing His Father.

Joy comes from our delicious and delightful relationship with Jesus; and with one another in the Body of Christ.

God wants us to walk in His joy! Jesus is saying, *"Father, I want more than anything for your children to be able to see You as I see You, to see You in Your goodness, mercy, and kindness."* When the Bible says that God inhabits and delights in the praises of His people (Ps. 22:3), it means that God whirls around in a dance! Perhaps that's what Jesus saw. I would imagine that as Jesus went about ministering, the Father rejoiced. *"Look at my Boy go! Touchdown, Jesus!"*

Here then is what God wants for us: righteousness, and peace, which leads us into His joy. Joy comes from our delicious and delightful relationship with Jesus; and with one another in the Body of Christ. What, then, are some of the characteristics of joy, and how is it received and maintained?

Our joy comes from our justification. We have been made right with the Lord.

> *"It is God that justifies"* (Rom 8:33).

We are no longer under judgment. We have been accepted in the beloved, and no man can take us out of His hands.

> *"There is therefore now no condemnation to them which are in Christ Jesus"* (Rom 8:1). Oh, what Joy!

The church needs joy. Joy is one of the major manifestations of the present renewal. People are bursting into uproarious laughter. They cannot contain themselves. They might laugh for a half hour, hour, or two hours straight. In their laughter, many feel a release from the Holy Spirit, with healing and refreshing. Some will break into paroxysms of tears alternating with laughing. Others will be slain in the Spirit. It is reported that many wake from these experiences having been embraced by the Father's love, perhaps seeing visions and experiencing dreams. At best, God is allowing many to experience the delight of the Lord, achieved through simple child-like faith.

Of course, the Kingdom is likened to child-like faith. Kids do not mind dancing and kicking up their feet, shouting, and loving each other. They don't ask, "I wonder what others think about me?" They just respond to their inner prompting.

When I was a child, my dad would occasionally take time to talk to me about some topic. These rare times were so special that I would start to giggle. Sometimes I'd break into laughter. I couldn't help it. He'd say, "What're you laughing at?" "I don't know, I'm just laughing." I was. I felt so honored, privileged, and blessed to be in the presence of my father, to receive, hear him, and have a relationship with him. That is the way kids are. When the teacher walks by, strokes them on the head and says, "You're doing a great job!' they giggle. They cannot help themselves. It is not contrived; nobody manipulates or whips it up. At best, God is allowing many to experience the delight of the Lord, achieved through simple child-like faith. Sadly, for many this experience of joy (which God intends for us to have as a part of our walk with God) has become the focus of worship, rather than an outgrowth of a maturing relationship with Christ. Do we seek joy for self or because we need joy (which is our strength) to fulfill our Kingdom mandate? Balance and wisdom are needed. Children have that naturally, but we take it out of them as adults. We break them of it and teach them to be appropriate, religious. God is taking us back into a dimension of pure delight before the Lord. It is the Holy Spirit that is bubbling up inside, which is to be experienced with decency and order.

Our expression probably should not be overly done in the workplace, or in the middle of a classroom. That might provide a ticket straight to the funny farm. But in your prayer closet, in your church, in your Bible study, in your relationships at home with your family, the expression of joy demonstrates that the Kingdom of God has come to you.

"We have substituted relativity for reality, psychology for prayer, an inferiority complex for sin, social control for family worship, auto suggestion for conversion, reflex action for revelation, the spirit of wheels for the power of the Spirit."

- Hugh Thomson Kerr

Chapter IX
Character of the Kingdom:
In The Holy Ghost

On the day of Pentecost, the Apostle Peter referenced the event of the Coming of The Holy Spirit as that which had been prophesied by Joel

> *"and it shall be in the last days; God says that I will pour faith of my spirit upon all mankind, and your son's and your daughters shall prophesy, and your young men shall see visions, and your old men shall dream dreams. Even upon my bondslaves, both men and women, I will in these days pour forth my Spirit."* Acts 2:17, 18, Joel 2:20-32.

The out pouring of The Holy Spirit, The Third Person of the Trinity, on the day of Pentecost, prophesied by Joel, Zechariah (4:6) and Jesus (Luke 24:49) among others, had significance to us on several accounts.

In The Holy Spirit alone is true Christian community.

First, His coming signified a major shift in God's dealing with mankind. Until Pentecost, The Holy Spirit was active in creation (Gen. 1:102), empowered men and women for service (i.e., see Sampson, Gideon, Daniel, etc.) and spoke through prophets particularly the purpose of God by way of inspiration. Jesus, emptied of divinity (Phil. 3) was filled with

The Holy Spirit without measure, was lead of The Spirit and functioned in the Power of The Spirit (Luke 4). Now, on the day of Pentecost, the work of The Holy Spirit was transferred from a specific people group (The Jew's) to the whole world, and the presence of God no longer came upon people only, but would dwell in people who put their faith and trust in Jesus Christ as God's provision for sin.

Secondly, the outpouring of The Holy Spirit began the "last days", inaugurating the Kingdom of God in the earth, and administrating the purposes of God through the church, by the gifts of Christ contained in The Holy Spirit. (Eph. 4) As the administrator of the purposes of God, The Holy Spirit brings us into relationship with The Father and The Son, gives us power and authority to live as God intended, provides care and comfort for us (John 14:15-18), teaches us all things and helps us remember (John 14:26), convicts us of righteousness, sin and judgment.

In The Holy Spirit, every area of life is transformed by The Spirit of God and the Word of God. The purpose of Messiah's Kingdom is to bring God's transformation, and the church, empowered by The Holy Spirit, is the instrument for the fulfillment of God's Eternal Purpose. The Spirit is the anointing, He is the supernatural empowerment.

Thus, when we speak of "in the Holy Ghost" the Apostle Paul assumed the readers understanding that there is no life, no righteousness, no peace, no joy, outside of the indwelling Spirit.

The indwelling of The Spirit gives opportunity and power to live right with God and others, enjoy the blessed peace that passes all understanding and provides new wine, joy unspeakable and full of glory. In The Holy Spirit alone is true Christian community. In The Holy Spirit we find the gifts (empowerments) which allow us to live triumphantly. In The Holy Spirit is God's government or rule, always pointing us to Christ, to fulfill the will of The Father. It is in The Holy Spirit that we experience the Character of God manifested in our lives, the fruit of The Spirit, which is love personified.

In Summary

Righteousness, peace, and joy should rule our conduct. When you think righteously and live uprightly, it demonstrates that the Kingdom of God has come into your house.

There is a rest for the people of God. At times we may have to struggle for it.

> *"Let us labor therefore to enter into that rest"* (Heb. 4:11).

When we can stand in the peace of Jesus in the midst of difficulties, because we know that

> *"All things work together for good to those that love God and are called according to His purpose"* (Rom. 8:28);

then we know that God's hand, his good hand, is upon our life and we will have His peace. It will show. It will demonstrate to the world that the Kingdom of God is in our family.

I don't mean the false peace that you find in eastern religion nor the empty feeling of peace in many Cultic families. You might sense a calm, an absence of fighting, but there is no relationship. It is a false peace. Rather, I am talking about the peace that passes understanding (Phil. 4:7). It has been imparted to us, and it shows that the Kingdom of God is here. Then we will show the joy of the Lord, which is our strength.

Joy. People ask me all the time, "What are you smiling about?" I answer, "I don't know, I'm alive, not dead. I'm breathing, it's a good day!" As far as I am concerned, every day we have to serve the Lord, that is a great day! I am able to get up, do what God has asked me to do, live a day in His presence; that is a good day! Don't sweat the small stuff. Be joyous. Take delight in God.

If we will delight ourselves in the Lord, He will give us the desires of our heart (Ps. 37:4). Not only will He place His desires in our heart, but He'll then bring out of our hearts those very delights.

Has sin or condemnation robbed you of righteousness? Deal with it quickly. How? Confess your sin. In some cases, we may have to make some restitution. We need to be right with others.

Sometimes we have to change our lifestyle. If you are a couch potato, get off the couch. If you are lazy, yet constantly nagging and yelling at your kids to do all the work, you probably need to get right with God. If you are a racist, you had better deal with that, for God hates racism.

You have to make things right. It's more than, "Father, forgive me because I hate sister So-N-So. And thank You for your forgiveness. See, I confessed it, so it's all OK." Then you spend the rest of your life avoiding sister So-N-So because you can't stand her. That is not forgiveness. Nothing is made right. You are walking in your sin and justifying it.

Perhaps there is still unsettled business in your life. Uncertainty in terms of one's future or direction of life can rob one of peace, even when one is living right with God. In the unsettled times, all you can do is to

> *"trust in the Lord with all your heart, and lean not on your own understanding; in all your ways acknowledge Him, and He will direct your path"* (Prov. 3:5-6).

"I guess I just have to trust you, Lord." It shouldn't be that hard as believers, but at times it is. We, especially those of us from Western descent, like being independent. We do not like being out of control. We want to be in control of everything. But truly, the only One in control of everything is God. When we cooperate with Him, we function at our best.

If people easily steal your peace from you, learn to set boundaries. Surround yourself with loving people. This is not to say do not minister to those who are weaker. If you can do so without losing your peace, praise God! You will be a peacemaker, for which there is blessing. But if you cannot minister without feeling like they've driven you mad, then perhaps you need to pass them on to someone else who can minister to them. I know I can't minister to everybody who walks on the face of the earth. There are certain ones about whom I yell, "Help!" I don't feel guilty about asking someone else to come alongside and minister. My responsibility is to get them the help they need, not to be their Messiah. So sometimes we have to set those boundaries, so we may walk in His peace.

Ultimately God wants us to experience His joy, to delight in the Lord. My parents would occasionally kick up their heels and dance to the music of Lawrence Welk. We kids would look on and laugh! It was wonderful. They were expressing their love for each other. Sometimes they would even become amorous, doing a little romantic hugging and kissing. We knew they were loving each other, and that gave us a greater sense of security. It provided us a sense that things were going to be alright. Our parents gave us hope. In the body of Christ we feel hope when we see those who experience the joy of the Lord, who are able to love each other, and who walk beside each other in difficult times. Hope arises in us that we too can enjoy the life God has given us!

Many of you can be models of the joy of the Lord. Hopefully, you don't have to plaster a smile on your face when you come into God's House (or more importantly, in the market place). Your smile flows naturally because the joy of the Lord resides in your heart. Your joyful smile says, "I'm so glad to see you! How was your week? Man, my week was terrible, but God is good! We're here together, and we're going to have a wonderful time, glory to Jesus." It lifts us all.

Imagine; when we all begin to delight ourselves in the Lord and allow His joy to flow through us, it will transform us! We will become strong as a Body! I would venture to say, we would be almost invincible. The devil can attack all he wants; when the joy of the Lord is flowing through us. We can live in victory. Paul stated,

> *"But thanks be to God, who always leads us in His triumph in Christ, and manifest through us the sweet aroma of the knowledge of Him in every place"* (2 Cor. 2:14).

Live right with God! If any person, situation or circumstance, if anything keeps you from walking in right relationship with God, why in your right mind would you hold on to it? Get rid of it! Lay it down! Repent! Change your thinking. Get right, and walk uprightly! That is the only way for God to be able to impart to you His peace and His joy.

There is much tribulation in the world. The righteousness of God and His Kingdom is all around us. It is in us. It is not a static kingdom or an organization, but it is an organism. The Kingdom is alive. It is constantly being expressed, constantly forcing men and women to face the truth about their lives. It challenges us to go far beyond where we ever thought we were capable of going. The Kingdom of God is constantly stretching and it will continue to do so until Jesus comes to establish His Kingdom fully and finally here on earth.

References

1. Bannerman, D. *The Scripture Doctrine of the Church.* Wm. B. Eerdmans Publishing Co. Grand Rapids, MI, 1955, pp. 249-250.

2. Bright, John. *The Kingdom of God.* Abingdon Press. Nashville, TN, 1981.

3. I bid

4. Galloway, and Galloway.

5. Hoffman, Mark. *On Earth As It Is In Heaven.* CSN. El Cajon, CA, 2003.

6. Ladd, George. *The Gospel of the Kingdom: Scriptural Studies in the Kingdom of God.* Wm. B. Eerdmans Publishing Co. Grand Rapids, MI, 1959.

7. Whyte, Peter. *The King and His Kingdom.* PI, 1989.

8. Zarn, Raymond, *Church and Kingdom.* Presbyterian and Reformed Publication. Philadelphia, PA 1962.

About the author

Dr. Stan DeKoven is a licensed Marriage, Family and Child Counselor in California, working for many years in the field. He is the Founder and President of the Vision International Network, with programs including Vision International University and Vision Bible College, and their Network of Campuses worldwide, Vision Publishing, The American Society of Christian Therapist and the Family Care Network. He is the author of over 30 books in practical Christian living for the maturing of God's people. Dr. DeKoven is married to his beautiful wife Noreen, and has two daughters, Rebecca and Rachel.

Other helpful books by Dr. DeKoven include:

Assessment of Human Needs
Christian Education
Family Violence: Patterns of Destruction
40 Days to the Promise
Fresh Manna
Grief Relief
The Healing Community
I Want To Be Like You Dad
Journey Through the New Testament
Journey Through the Old Testament
Journey to Wholeness
Leadership: Vision for the City
Living Fruitfully
Marriage and Family Life
New Beginnings
On Belay! Introduction to Christian Counseling
Parenting on Purpose
Pastoral Ministry
Research Writing made Easy
Starting Out Right
Substance Abuse Therapy
Supernatural Architecture
Turning Points
Twelve Steps to Wholeness

www.ingramcontent.com/pod-product-compliance
Lightning Source LLC
LaVergne TN
LVHW090047090426
835511LV00031B/417